Easy Classical Masterworks for Viola

Easy Classical Masterworks for Viola

Music of Bach, Beethoven, Brahms, Handel, Haydn, Mozart, Schubert, Tchaikovsky, Vivaldi and Wagner

Easy Classical Masterworks for Viola

© Easy Classical Masterworks

ISBN-13:978-1499174687
ISBN-10:1499174683

Bach
Bourrée, BWV 996 9
Gavotte II, BWV 808 10
Menuett, BWV Anh 114 11

Beethoven
Chorfantasie Op. 80 15
Für Elise, WoO 59 16
Ode an die Freude, Op. 125 17

Brahms
Ungarischen Tänze N° 5, WoO 1 21
Poco allegretto 3. Sinfonie F-Dur, op. 90 22
Guten Abend, gut' Nacht 23

Handel
Sarabande, HWV 437 27
Hallelujah, HWV 56 28
Water Music, HWV 349 29

Haydn
Sinfonie Nr. 94 G-Dur, Hob.I:94 33

Mozart
"Ah vous dirais-je, Maman", K. 265 37
Rondo Alla Turca, K. 331 38
40. Sinfonie, K.550 39

Schubert
Ständchen, D.957 43

Tchaikovsky
Dance of the Sugar Plum Fairy, Op. 71a 47
March, Op. 71a 48
Sleeping Beauty Waltz, Op.66a 49

Vivaldi
la Primavera, RV. 269 53
l'Estate, RV. 315 54
l'Autunno, RV. 293 55
l'Inverno, RV. 297 56

Wagner
Tannhäuser Ouvertüre, WWV 70 59

Bourrée, BWV 996

Johann Sebastian Bach

Gavotte II, BWV 808

Johann Sebastian Bach

Menuett, BWV Anh 114

Johann Sebastian Bach

Chorfantasie, Op. 80

Ludwig van Beethoven

Für Elise, WoO 59

Ludwig van Beethoven

Ode an die Freude, Op. 125

Ludwig van Beethoven

Allegro

Ungarischen Tänze Nº 5, WoO 1

Johannes Brahms

3. Sinfonie F-Dur, op. 90

Johannes Brahms

Poco allegretto

Guten Abend, gut' Nacht

Johannes Brahms

GEORGE HAENDEL

Sarabande, HWV 437

George Frideric Handel

Hallelujah, HWV 56

George Frideric Handel

Water Music, HWV 349

George Frideric Handel

Alla Hornpipe

Sinfonie Nr. 94 G-Dur, Hob.I:94
"mit dem Paukenschlag"

Joseph Haydn

Ah vous dirais-je, Maman

Wolfgang Amadeus Mozart

Rondo Alla Turca, K. 331

Wolfgang Amadeus Mozart

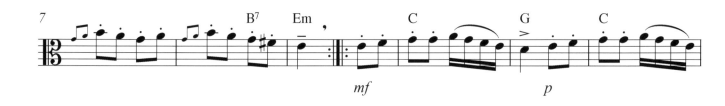

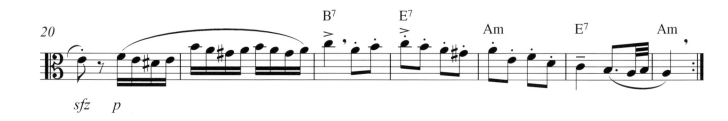

40. Sinfonie, K.550

Wolfgang Amadeus Mozart

Allegro molto

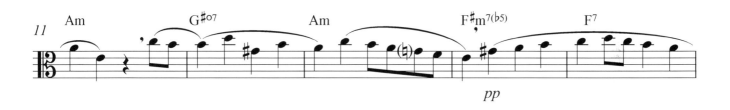
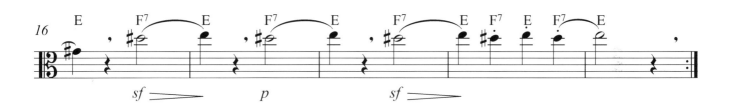

Ständchen, D.957

Franz Schubert

Щелкунчик, Op. 71a

(Dance of the Sugar Plum Fairy)

Piotr Ilyich Tchaikovsky

Щелкунчик, Op. 71a

(March of The Nutcracker)

Piotr Ilyich Tchaikovsky

Спящая красавица, Op.66a

(Sleeping Beauty Waltz)

Piotr Ilyich Tchaikovsky

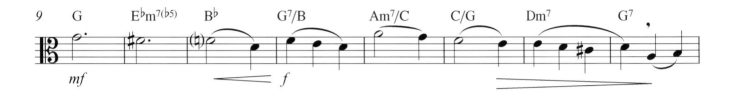

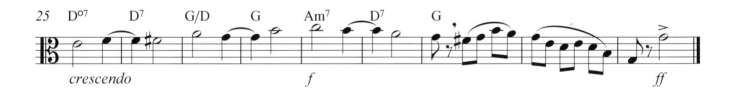

ANTONIO VIVALDI

la Primavera, RV. 269

Antonio Vivaldi

l'Estate, RV. 315

Antonio Vivaldi

Allegro non molto

l'Autunno, RV. 293

Antonio Vivaldi

l'Inverno, RV. 297

Antonio Vivaldi

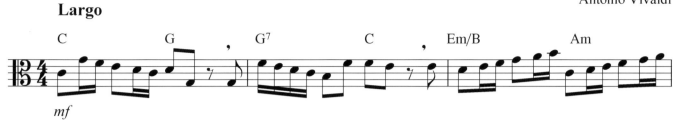

Tannhäuser Ouvertüre, WWV 70

Richard Wagner

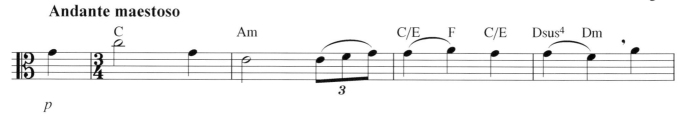
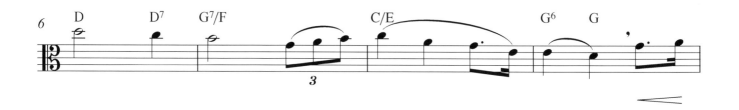

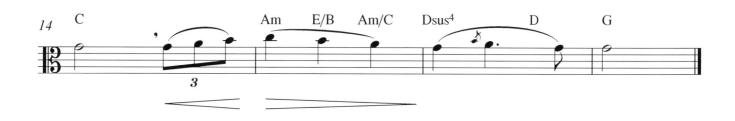

Made in the USA
Middletown, DE
30 December 2016